Family Name

_____

Date

_____

OUR FAMILY STORY

A Keepsake Book

Donna Shryer

new seasons®

Donna Shryer lives in Chicago, Illinois, where she writes and enjoys everything about family—past as well as present.

Illustration by Ken Call

Photo credits:
Sara Ewald: 23; Patricia Ulrich/Cynthia Sacks: 49; Raffel Youngman: 45.

New Seasons is a registered trademark of Publications International, Ltd.

Louis Weber, CEO
Publications International, Ltd.
7373 North Cicero Avenue
Lincolnwood, Illinois 60712

www.pilbooks.com

Permission is never granted for commercial purposes.

Manufactured in China.

8 7 6 5 4 3 2 1

ISBN-13: 978-1-4127-5394-4
ISBN-10: 1-4127-5394-5

Contents

A Trip Down Memory Lane

You are about to embark on a marvelous journey. Yet with all its magnificence, this journey costs nothing and involves no reservations or luggage. Best of all, this experience is unique, for it is *your* family story.

While this particular trip is best taken from a cozy chair in the comfort of your own home, you will be traveling—back to joyous memories. This is a rare opportunity to reminisce about events and people and to rediscover thoughts long misplaced in the back of your mind.

Generations to come will cherish this historical, insightful, and highly entertaining book. Within your recorded notes and stories will be a valuable key to the family's past and present as well as a glimpse into the future. Remember, a family story is part happenstance, part tradition, and part genetics! Your children's grandchildren might one day read your story and claim with delight, "Now I know where I got my love of music—from my great-grandmother."

Once you begin this project, you will see how simple it is. Thoughtful questions lead the way and take you to the precise memories your family will most want to read. Sometimes these questions are straightforward, asking for birthdays or anniversary dates. Other times they will prompt you to describe loved ones or special feelings associated with a treasured family tradition.

To help you fully enjoy this experience, here are a few helpful hints.

- When joining relatives for dinner, be sure to pack your family's favorite recipe and this book. After everyone's done eating, pull out *Our Family Story* and enlist the group's help. It's a terrific way to answer questions that leave you stymied and a wonderful occasion to bring the family closer together.

- Take your time, and relish each entry. You may even bump into a few memories that do not belong in this book. That's fine! Enjoy them. And know that they may direct you to other memories that do belong on these pages.

- Every family history is unique, so some questions simply will not apply to your family. This book covers a lot of possible twists and turns in your past. Either skip these questions (guilt free!), or complete the questions by interviewing someone else—perhaps your spouse, a brother, or another family member who has a story to tell.

- When appropriate, try to include interesting details about the time period of a noted memory. For example, does a memory about a special person trace back to the Great Depression and rationing? Or, when mentioning a radio program that you loved, be sure to include the fact that television was not yet around. Your grandchildren, who think all-day cartoons and music videos are a natural part of life, will love reading this tidbit!

- Not every notation needs a long story, but if you are so inclined, continue onto a separate piece of paper. Staple this paper to the page that triggered your longer recollection.

- Finally, you may find yourself quite smitten with your own family story! Once you begin this project, you may experience a steady stream of memories at all times of the day and night. With this in mind, keep a small pad of paper and a pen on your nightstand, tucked in your purse or briefcase, and in the car. Then when you sink into that cozy chair in the comfort of your own home, you'll have these spontaneous memories close at hand.

So, are you ready to begin your journey? Turn the page and get ready for the experience of your life!

Family Ties

Think of this section as your family tree in sentence format,
giving generations to come the story of their origins.

Me, Myself, and I

What is your full name? _____

_____

Do you have any information about your last name? Does it mean something in
another language? Is the current spelling and pronunciation of your last name just as
your ancestors spelled and pronounced it? _____

_____

_____

_____

_____

_____

In what city and state were you born? _____

_____

When is your birthday? Where and at what time were you born? _____

_____

_____

Did your parents share any stories about your birth? If so, write one here:

Are you named after anyone? Is there a story behind your name?

Do you have a nickname? Who gave it to you, and why? How did you feel about this nickname while growing up? Do people still use your nickname?

Grand Beginnings

*Use the boxes below and on page 13 to answer the following questions
about each of your grandparents.*

What is this grandparent's full name? In what year was he or she born? Where was
this grandparent born? If born in another country, in what year did he or she come
to America? If born in the United States, what generation American are they? What
did you call this grandparent? If something other than the traditional Grandma or
Grandpa, what is the story behind this name? What special memory do you have
about this grandparent?

Mother Dear

What is your mother's full name? _____

_____

When was she born? _____

_____

Where was your mom born? If she was born in another country, how old was she when she arrived in America, and how did she come here? Did she travel with family or alone? _____

_____

_____

_____

Did your mom tell you any stories about her childhood? Please share them. _____

_____

_____

_____

What is the greatest piece of advice your mother gave you? _____

_____

_____

_____

Place your mother's photo here.

What do you admire most about your mom? _____

_____

_____

_____

Father of Mine

What is your father's full name? _____

_____

When was he born? _____

_____

Where was your father born? If born in another
country, when and how did he come to America?
Did he travel with family or alone? _____

_____

_____

_____

*Place your father's
photo here.*

What is your dad's favorite and most often repeated
story about his childhood? _____

_____

_____

What's the greatest piece of advice your father gave you? _____

_____

_____

What do you admire most about your father? _____

_____

_____

Brotherly and Sisterly Love

How many brothers and sisters do you have? Where do you fall in the birth order?

_____

_____

What are your siblings' names and birthdays?

_____

_____

_____

_____

_____

_____

_____

What are the names of your siblings' spouses and children? Note your siblings'
anniversary dates and your nieces' and nephews' birthdays, too.

_____

_____

_____

_____

_____

_____

_____

What activity did you most enjoy sharing with your siblings?

_____

_____

_____

_____

_____

_____

_____

What would cause a squabble to break out between you and your brothers and sisters?

_____

_____

_____

_____

_____

_____

My Other Half

What is your spouse's full name? _____

_____

Is your spouse named after anyone? Is there a story behind the name? _____

_____

_____

_____

_____

Does your spouse have a nickname? Do you have any pet names for your spouse?

_____

_____

_____

Where was your spouse born? _____

_____

When is your spouse's birthday? _____

_____

Who proposed to whom? Describe the proposal. _____

_____

_____

_____

_____

When and where were you married? What was the wedding like?

_____

_____

_____

_____

_____

_____

_____

_____

_____

_____

What is your fondest memory of your first year
of marriage? _____

_____

_____

_____

_____

_____

_____

_____

_____

_____

_____

*Place your wedding
photo here.*

Branching Out

Use the boxes below and on page 21 to answer the following questions about your spouse's parents and grandparents.

What is this person's full name? When and where was he or she born? What special memory do you or your spouse have about this person?

Little Chips off the Old Block

How many children do you have, and what are their names?

When is each child's birthday?

Tell one story about each child's birth.

How is each child most like you? How is each child most like your spouse?

Can you describe the most rewarding part about being a parent? How about the most challenging part?

If any of your children are married, what is the name of each child's spouse?

The Greatest Grandkids

How many grandchildren do you have, and what are their names?

_____

_____

_____

_____

When is each grandchild's birthday?

_____

_____

_____

What do your grandchildren call you? Are there any traditions in your family as to what grandparents are called? How did this tradition begin?

_____

_____

_____

_____

What is the most wonderful part about being a grandparent?

_____

_____

_____

_____

Pooling Your Resources

What is a dominant family trait that every parent in your family hopes to pass on?

When people say to your children, "You're just like your mother!" what are they usually referring to?

What about you is most like your own mother? What is most like your father?

Is there a dominant physical feature in your family, such as red hair, freckles, or height?

Childhood Stories

This is your chance to record special childhood memories as well as to provide a quick glance at the world in which you grew up.

There's No Place Like Home

Where was your childhood home, and how long did you live there? Can you still remember the address and phone number?

_____

_____

_____

_____

What did your house and yard look like? How many rooms were there? How many bathrooms did it have? Try to include details, such as if you had a yard, electricity, indoor plumbing, or a telephone.

_____

_____

_____

_____

_____

_____

_____

Do you remember your childhood bedroom? Did you share the room with a sister or brother? What color was it?

Can you remember any household chores that were your responsibility?

Where did the family normally eat dinner? Describe a typical dinner during your childhood years.

Neighborly Thoughts

What was your childhood neighborhood like? Can you describe any memorable neighbors? _____

_____

_____

_____

Was there one dominant ethnic or religious group in this neighborhood or was it diverse? Explain. _____

_____

_____

_____

Were there any shops in your neighborhood that you loved to visit as a kid? What about restaurants? _____

_____

_____

_____

Did neighbors ever get together for parties? If so, what were these get-togethers like? _____

_____

_____

_____

Friends Are Forever

Who was your best friend growing up? How and where did you meet this friend?

_____

_____

_____

_____

What did you most enjoy playing with him or her?

_____

_____

_____

_____

What was the most popular game you played with friends? Is this game still around? Did you ever play it with your children or grandchildren?

_____

_____

_____

_____

Are you still in contact with any childhood friends? What story do these friends like to tell about you?

_____

_____

_____

_____

Pet Tales

Did you have pets while growing up? If so, what kind of pets were they? _____

_____

_____

_____

What were your pets' names, and what's the story behind each name? _____

_____

_____

_____

Can you recall any funny stories about a particular pet? _____

_____

_____

_____

_____

_____

As a child, what were your responsibilities when it came to the care and feeding of the family pet? _____

_____

_____

What did you enjoy doing with your pet? _____

_____

_____

_____

Entertaining Memories

Do you remember your parents playing any record albums? If so, who was the artist and what sort of music was it? _____

_____

_____

Which television shows did you and your family watch? If you didn't have a TV, which radio programs did you listen to? _____

_____

_____

_____

What was a favorite book you remember reading? _____

_____

_____

_____

_____

Can you remember your favorite bedtime storybook? What was it about? _____

_____

_____

_____

_____

_____

What was the most popular movie when you were a child? Who were the top movie stars back then? How much did it cost to go to the movies?

What did you and your family do for fun when you were a child?

Did you have a hobby as a child? What was it, and do you still enjoy this hobby?

What was the hot toy when you were growing up? Do you still have this toy?

Political Point of View

Who was president when you were born, and what were the country's top concerns?

_____

_____

_____

_____

Can you name all the presidents who served during your lifetime?

_____

_____

_____

Is there one significant international or national event you remember from your childhood? What was it, and where were you when you heard the news?

_____

_____

_____

_____

What war did you live through as a child, and how did the country's involvement in this war shape your family life? Did you have relatives who served in the military during this war?

_____

_____

_____

_____

_____

To Be a Kid Again

What is your earliest memory? _____
_____
_____
_____
_____
_____

What is your fondest childhood memory? Who shared this memory with you?
_____
_____
_____
_____
_____
_____

If you could relive one event (or year) during your childhood, what would it be?
_____
_____
_____
_____
_____
_____

What did you look like as a child? What color hair did you have? Were you the tallest or the shortest in your class?

How did kids dress when you were a child? Be sure to include lots of details!

Did you receive an allowance as a child? How much did you get, and what did you most often spend your money on?

Did you have a hero when you were a child? Why did you look up to this person?

The Teen Scene

Every decade of teenagers has a trademark fad or trend. How did the teenagers of your day make their mark? Did your generation have a nickname, like the Bobby-Soxers or Generation X?

_____

_____

_____

_____

_____

What is your best memory as a teenager? _____

_____

_____

_____

_____

_____

Who was your favorite band or entertainer, and why? Did you ever see this person perform live?

_____

_____

_____

_____

How old were you when you started dating? What was a typical date like?

_____

_____

_____

_____

_____

Did you have a steady boyfriend or girlfriend? What did "going steady" mean?

What did you look like as a teenager? What was your hairstyle? How tall were you? How did you feel about the way you looked?

As a teenager, did you receive an allowance? If so, how much did you receive? How did you earn this money, and what did you usually spend it on?

Can you remember any phrases that were popular when you were a teenager? What did they mean?

Did you have a curfew as a teen? What was it?

School Days

As this section proves, education is so much more than reading, writing, and arithmetic!

Learning the Ropes

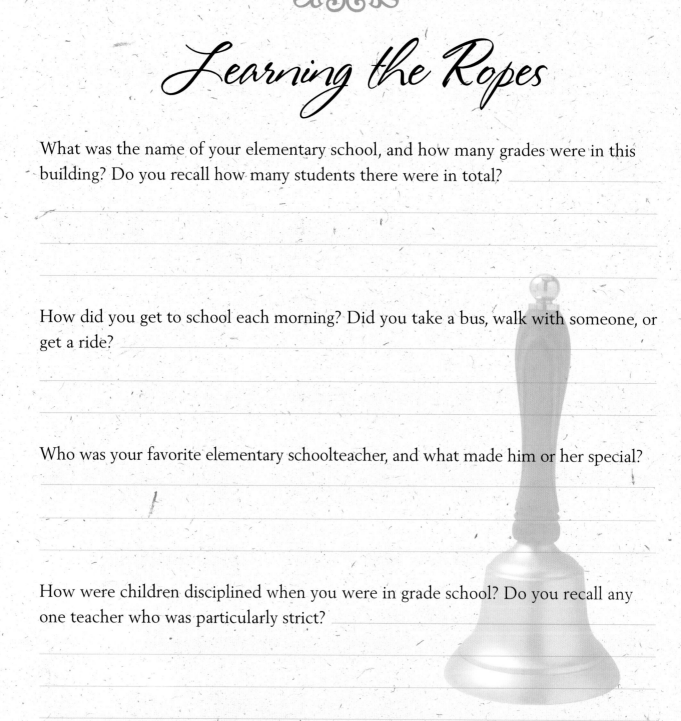

What was the name of your elementary school, and how many grades were in this building? Do you recall how many students there were in total?

_____

_____

How did you get to school each morning? Did you take a bus, walk with someone, or get a ride?

_____

_____

Who was your favorite elementary schoolteacher, and what made him or her special?

_____

_____

How were children disciplined when you were in grade school? Do you recall any one teacher who was particularly strict?

_____

_____

What was your favorite subject in elementary school? How about your least favorite?

What grades did you usually get?

How did you normally dress for school?

About what grade were you in when homework started? How did you carry your books to and from school—in a backpack, in your arms, or in some other fashion?

What were the favorite recess games when you were in elementary school?

Beyond classroom studies, what school activities did you most enjoy?

Did you have physical education as a youngster? If so, what games did you play and what was your favorite activity?

What was lunchtime like in your school? Did your school serve hot lunches? If so, what were they like and what was your favorite menu? Or, did you go home for lunch or bring a bag lunch to school?

Reaching Higher

Where did you go to high school? Do you remember how many students were in your graduating class?

How did you get to school each day?

Which high school teacher most influenced you? Why?

What was your favorite subject in high school? How about your least favorite? What sort of grades did you receive?

Did you have to take classes that are no longer mandatory today, like Home Ec or Shop? What sort of things did you learn?

How did you normally dress for school?

Can you remember any cliques in your high school? Can you describe the popular girls? What were the popular guys like?

Did you participate in any high school sports? If so, what were your favorites? Did you regularly attend any sporting events?

Beyond classroom studies, what school activities were you involved in?

Who did you normally eat lunch with? What did you usually talk about?

Did you attend your high school prom? What was it like? Do you remember your prom's theme or song?

Ivy-Covered Halls

What college did you attend, and why did you choose to go there? _____
_____
_____
_____
_____
_____
_____

How much was tuition, and how did you or your family pay for it? _____
_____
_____
_____
_____
_____
_____
_____

Was this a large or small college? Can you describe the campus? _____
_____
_____
_____
_____
_____
_____
_____

What was your major? Did you stick with your original major or change majors? Why did you select this major?

Who was the one professor that most influenced your life decisions? Describe how.

What was the one class that really opened your eyes and set the wheels in motion toward bigger things— perhaps a new major, a finely tuned career goal, or another important decision?

Did you ever live in a dormitory? What was it like? Can you describe the dorm rules, such as curfew or visits from the opposite sex? Who was your first roommate?

Beyond classroom studies, did you participate in any activities or join any clubs?

Were your college sports teams good? Did you attend the games? How would you and your friends typically celebrate a win?

Where did you and your friends like to hang out? What did you do for fun?

Looking back, what was the best part of your college days?

Family Holidays

Here's your chance to pass on wonderful family traditions associated with the holidays. Be generous with details, and include recipes when you can!

Giving Thanks for Tradition

Who do you normally share Thanksgiving with?

_____

_____

What does your family's Thanksgiving dinner include? Are there any unusual foods that your family always serves? If so, how did this tradition begin?

_____

_____

_____

What is your favorite Thanksgiving memory?

_____

_____

_____

_____

_____

_____

Wonderful Winter Holidays

What wintertime holiday does your family most look forward to? _____
_____
_____

Who traditionally shares this holiday and on what day (e.g., Christmas Eve, the last day of Chanukah, the first night of Kwanzaa, etc.)? _____
_____
_____
_____

What is your favorite childhood memory or story about this holiday? _____
_____
_____
_____
_____
_____
_____
_____
_____

What is the oldest family tradition associated with this holiday? Who started this tradition and why? Has this tradition been altered or expanded upon over time?

Why does this holiday have special meaning for your family?

What do the adults most enjoy about this holiday? How about the kids?

Are there any traditions when it comes to giving gifts?

What were the gifts like when you were young? How has gift-giving changed over time?

Celebrate!

What other holiday is important to your family? _____

_____

_____

_____

_____

_____

_____

Which family members traditionally gather for this holiday, and where do you celebrate? _____

_____

_____

_____

_____

_____

_____

Can you share a favorite childhood memory or story about this holiday? _____

_____

_____

_____

_____

_____

_____

_____

_____

When it comes to this holiday, which traditions did you most want to pass along to the next generation? _____

_____

_____

_____

_____

_____

_____

_____

_____

_____

Is there any special food you associate with this holiday? Can you share the recipe?

_____

_____

_____

_____

_____

_____

_____

_____

_____

_____

Traditions and Folklore

Many cherished traditions and tales are unique to your family—like an heirloom christening gown or birthday party customs. This is your chance to note all of it for future generations.

Vacation Memories

What were family vacations like when you were a child? _____
_____
_____
_____
_____
_____
_____

While growing up, did your family ever return to a particular vacation spot again and again? Did you continue this tradition with your children? What is your most special memory of this place? _____
_____
_____
_____
_____
_____

What was a favorite vacation you took with your own family? What is your most special memory of this trip?

_____

_____

_____

_____

_____

_____

_____

_____

_____

Can you share one vacation-related tale that your family loves to tell?

_____

_____

_____

_____

_____

_____

_____

_____

_____

_____

_____

_____

Summer Fun

School's out! As a child, what did you do for fun during the summer? _____

_____

_____

_____

_____

_____

_____

_____

_____

_____

_____

What's the biggest difference between summertime fun for kids today compared to your childhood? _____

_____

_____

_____

_____

_____

_____

_____

_____

_____

Did you go to camp as a child? If so, what was the camp's name, and where was it located? How many years did you attend this camp?

Did you ever share a camp story with your children—a tale that made them want to attend camp? What's the story?

Family Reconnections

Does your family come together for a reunion? If so, where is it traditionally held? How often does this event occur? Which family members share this tradition? Who travels the farthest to attend?

_____

_____

_____

_____

_____

What about the reunion do you most look forward to? _____

_____

_____

_____

_____

What story about this family event is told over and over but never gets old? _____

_____

_____

_____

_____

_____

Can you recall the most emotional family reunion, perhaps because a loved one returned safely from war or you met a new family addition for the first time?

Food is a huge part of family reunions. Can you describe a typical spread? Which treat do you most look forward to, and who makes it?

Is there a traditional game, activity, or competition at your family reunions? Who usually wins this event?

Happy Birthday to You!

Does your family celebrate birthdays with any special tradition? What is it?

_____

_____

_____

_____

_____

_____

_____

_____

_____

_____

What were birthday parties like when you were a child? How are your children's or grandchildren's parties different?

_____

_____

_____

_____

_____

_____

_____

_____

_____

_____

_____

Does one particular birthday celebration stand out in your memory—be it your own, a child's, or a grandchild's? What about this celebration made it special? _____

_____

_____

_____

_____

_____

What was your most memorable birthday gift as a child? _____

_____

_____

Do you have a gift-buying tradition with any children or grandchildren? _____

_____

_____

_____

Is there a special birthday cake recipe? Who traditionally bakes this cake? Can you share the recipe? _____

_____

_____

_____

_____

_____

_____

_____

_____

Weekly Wonders

Did you have any weekly family traditions while growing up, like going to Grandma's house for Sunday dinner or baking with Mom? What's your fondest memory about this event?

_____

_____

_____

_____

_____

_____

_____

_____

Do you continue this tradition today? If so, with whom do you share it?

_____

_____

_____

_____

_____

_____

_____

_____

Spiritual Richness

What religion are you? Is this the same religion you grew up with? _____
_____
_____

How important was religion in your childhood home? How about in your adult
home? _____
_____
_____

Did you raise your children with this religion? Have any of your children or grandchildren chosen to follow a different religion? _____
_____
_____
_____

When a baby is born in your family, what religious ceremonies are performed? Can
you share a story connected to this event? _____
_____
_____
_____

When there is a marriage in your family, what religious traditions are honored? Can
you describe them? _____
_____
_____
_____

And the Title Goes To...

According to family reputation, tradition, and, of course, legendary folklore, assign a family member's name to each of the following titles. Remember... this is all in good fun!

Advice columnist in waiting: _____

Animal fan: _____

Artist: _____

Blue-ribbon baker: _____

Cuddle expert: _____

Diva: _____

Drama king or queen: _____

Favorite photographer: _____

First-place athlete: _____

Friend to all: _____

Gold-medal cook: _____

Green thumb: _____

Honorary beauty pageant winner: _____

Inventive genius: _____

Knee-slappin' comic: _____

Legendary storyteller: _____

Most creative mind: _____

Penny-pincher: _____

Political activist: _____

Prankster: _____

Problem solver: _____

White-glove housekeeper: _____

Wild child (age is irrelevant): _____

Tall Tales, Big Laughs

What is your favorite family story? Why do you love reciting or hearing this story?

_____

_____

_____

_____

_____

_____

_____

_____

_____

_____

What story do your children enjoy repeating…much to your chagrin?

_____

_____

_____

_____

_____

_____

_____

_____

What story do you like to tell about your children...much to their dismay?

Is there or has there ever been a famous—or infamous—person in your family? How did this person earn such notoriety?

9 to 5 and Beyond

Give future generations a flavor for past work environments—be it corporate or military—by completing the questions in this section.

It's a Family Affair

Is there or was there ever a family-owned business that adult children naturally went into? Can you describe this business? _____

_____

_____

_____

_____

_____

Did you go into this business? Did or will your children go into this family business? How do they feel about this professional heritage? _____

_____

_____

_____

_____

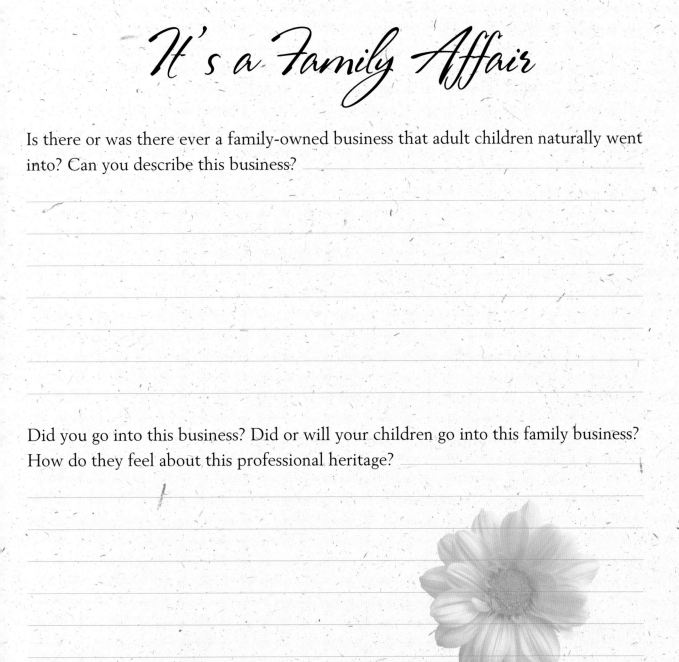

Can you give a few details about the history of this family business—how it began, how it changed over the years?

If there was no family-owned business, what did your great-grandfather do for a living? What about your grandfather? Did any family members make similar career choices?

Daddy's Home!

What did your father do for a living? Did you ever visit his workplace? What did you think about your father's career?

Did your dad have great loyalty for one particular company? If so, what was the company's name, and how many years did he work for this company? If not, how often did he change companies, and why?

When you imagine your father going off to work each morning, how was he dressed?
Was this the typical dress code for working men back then?

In your childhood neighborhood, what percentage of fathers do you think were their
family's sole source of income?

What advice did your father give you about selecting a career?

Women's Work

Did your mom have a career outside the home? If so, what did she do, and for what company? _____

_____

_____

_____

_____

_____

_____

_____

_____

_____

If you had a stay-at-home mother, what did she do professionally before she had children? Did your mother eventually return to her profession? _____

_____

_____

_____

_____

What career choices were available to women when you were growing up? What about when you were a young adult? _____

_____

_____

_____

_____

_____

Was there a woman in your family history who bucked tradition and went on to achieve great things? What did she do? Did she face any roadblocks while pursuing her career?

_____

_____

_____

_____

_____

_____

_____

_____

_____

_____

_____

_____

_____

What advice did your mom give you on the subject of choosing a career?

_____

_____

_____

_____

_____

_____

_____

_____

_____

_____

_____

_____

Pocket Change

What was your first after-school job? Was this a typical job for people your age? At what age did you and your friends get jobs? _____

_____

_____

_____

Were you working for spending money or for a special purchase? On what did kids in your day usually spend their money? _____

_____

_____

_____

_____

Do you remember what your pay was? Was this a good rate at that time? _____

_____

_____

Did your paycheck go in your own pocket or did you contribute to any family expenses, such as a college fund or household necessities? _____

_____

_____

Did you ever babysit? What was the going rate? _____

_____

_____

Climbing the Corporate Ladder

What was your first career-related position? Did you begin your career right after high school, or did you go to college first?

_____

_____

_____

_____

_____

_____

_____

Did you remain in this field or did you change careers? If you changed career paths, what did you go on to do, and why?

_____

_____

_____

_____

_____

_____

_____

Can you describe what corporate life was like when you first started working? How have things changed, and which changes are for the better?

_____

_____

_____

_____

_____

Uncle Sam Wants You

Did you or anyone else in your family ever pursue a military career? In what branch of service? What was military service like?

_____

_____

_____

_____

_____

_____

_____

_____

_____

_____

What was the country's attitude toward its military system when you were a young adult? How and why have attitudes changed?

_____

_____

_____

_____

_____

_____

If a child or grandchild chose to join the military, how would you feel? What advice would you give this young adult?

_____

_____

_____

_____

_____

Family Medical Information

Heredity is linked to many diseases and conditions. Today, medical technology can often prevent these conditions from developing—but only if your family has a medical tree.

Note any family members who had the following diseases or conditions. Include significant dates, such as approximate date of diagnosis and how old the person was when diagnosed. Also include any known medical reason for the disease or condition.

Allergies, including asthma _____

Alzheimer's disease _____

Cancer (specify type) _____

Childbearing conditions _____

Cystic fibrosis _____

Depression, anxiety, or other psychiatric illness _____

Diabetes _____

Eye diseases _____

Hearing loss _____

Heart disease _____

High blood pressure _____

Huntington's disease _____

Learning disabilities or mental retardation _____

Parkinson's disease _____

Polycystic kidney disease (PKD) _____

Sickle cell anemia _____

Other _____

Final Words

Here's a chance to say all those things you've always wanted to say...but never did.

What one piece of advice would you like to pass on to future generations?

If you could live life all over again, what would you change?

Is there anything you would like to say to your children—something you've never said or perhaps do not say enough?